GOSPEL TREAS...

CONTENTS

— PIANO LEVEL —
EARLY INTERMEDIATE
(HLSPL LEVEL 4-5)

ISBN 978-0-634-03699-6

HAL•LEONARD®
CORPORATION

7777 W. BLUEMOUND RD. P.O. BOX 13819 MILWAUKEE. WI 53213

Visit Hal Leonard Online at
www.halleonard.com

PREFACE

I was raised in a small town in eastern Oregon named Vale. My family walked to church each Sunday morning, and it was late in my childhood before I realized that it was not *the* "little brown church in the vale" as described in "Church in the Wildwood." My church was actually white, not brown, but that didn't sway my assumption. This was the church where my faith was grounded, where I first heard most of the songs that are in this collection, and where I eventually married my wife. It was this congregation that joyously sang along with my initial attempts at hymn playing and encouraged me when I played my first piano solo. This was the community that gave me the positive feedback that blossomed into confidence in my own music-making potential…and made me aware that all good gifts come from God.

Yes, I believe I can assuredly say "no other spot is so dear to my childhood as the little *white* church in the vale." (Vale, Oregon, that is!) This book is dedicated to all those souls who formed the fabric of my early life in the Vale United Methodist Church.

> With a grateful heart,
> Phillip Keveren

BIOGRAPHY

Phillip Keveren, a multi-talented keyboard artist and composer, has composed original works in a variety of genres from piano solo to symphonic orchestra. Mr. Keveren gives frequent concerts and workshops for teachers and their students in the United States, Canada, Europe, and Asia. Mr. Keveren holds a B.M. in composition from California State University Northridge and a M.M. in composition from the University of Southern California.

ARE YOU WASHED IN THE BLOOD?

Words and Music by ELISHA A. HOFFMAN
Arranged by Phillip Keveren

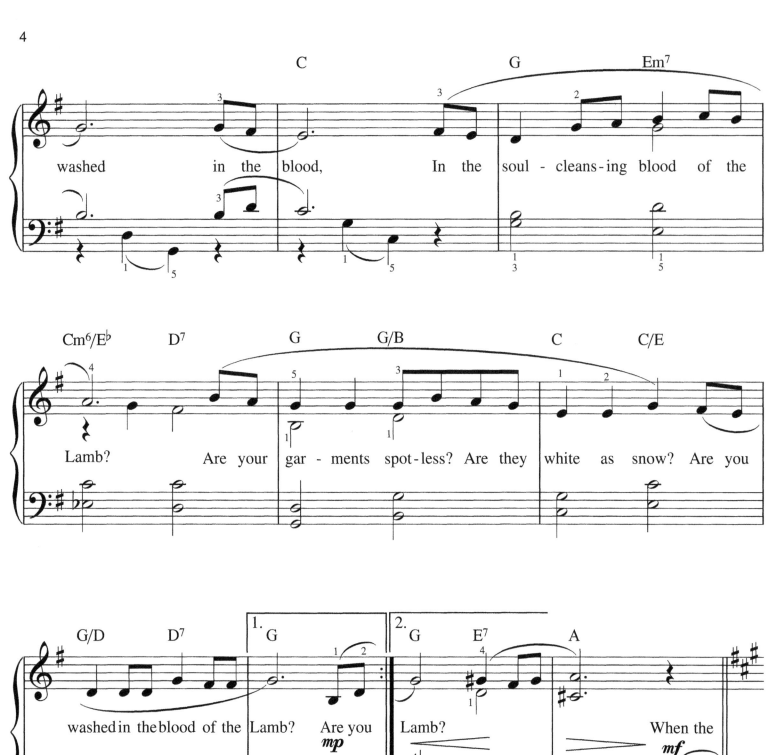

AMAZING GRACE

Words by JOHN NEWTON
Traditional American Melody
Arranged by Phillip Keveren

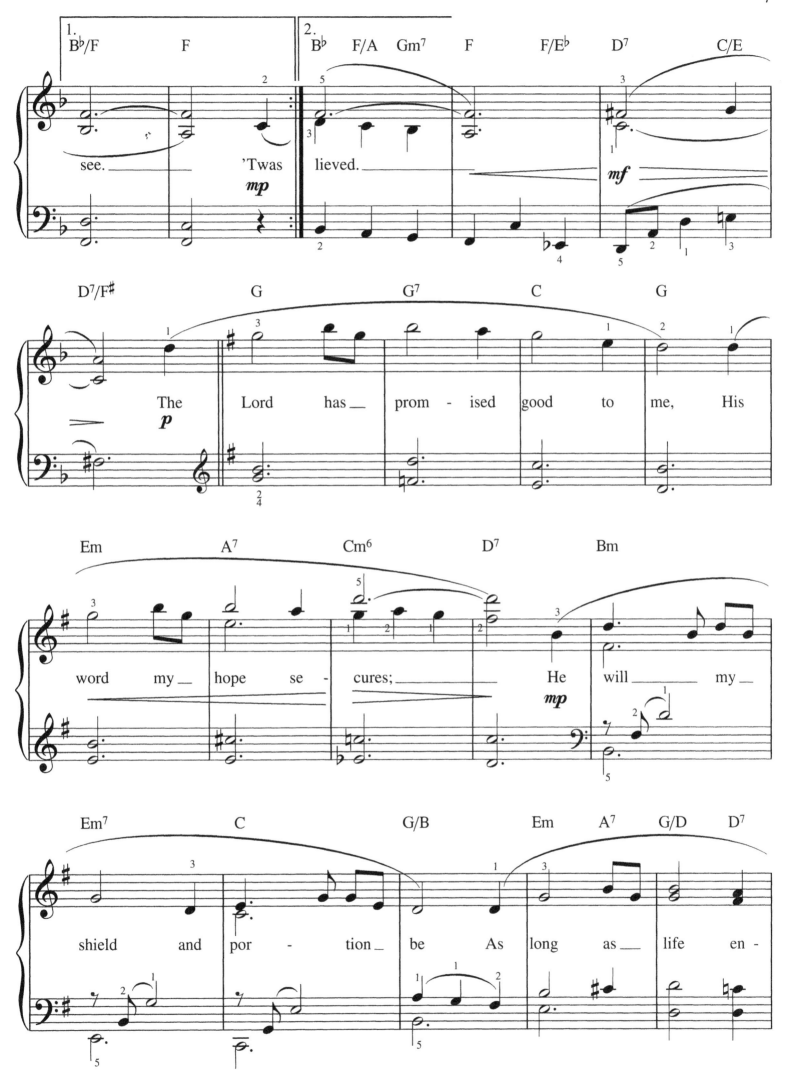

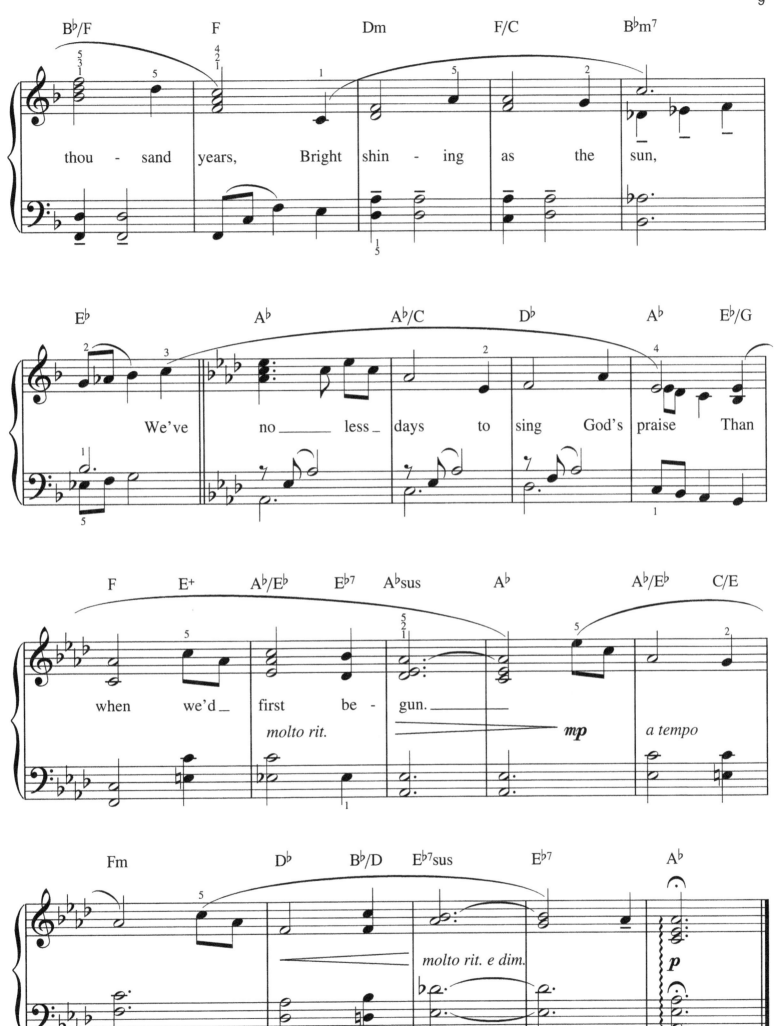

AT CALVARY

Words by WILLIAM R. NEWELL
Music by DANIEL B. TOWNER
Arranged by Phillip Keveren

grace was free; Par - don there was mul - ti - plied to me;

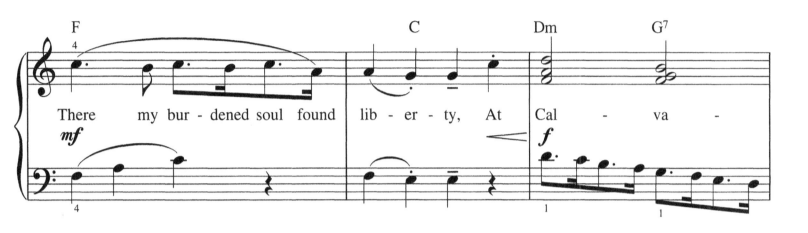

There my bur - dened soul found lib - er - ty, At Cal - va -

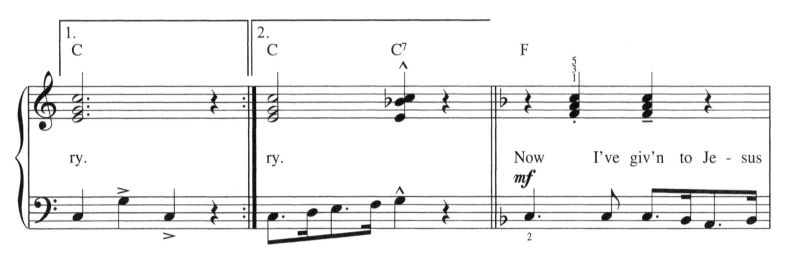

ry. ry. Now I've giv'n to Je - sus

ev - 'ry - thing; Now I glad - ly own Him as my King;

12

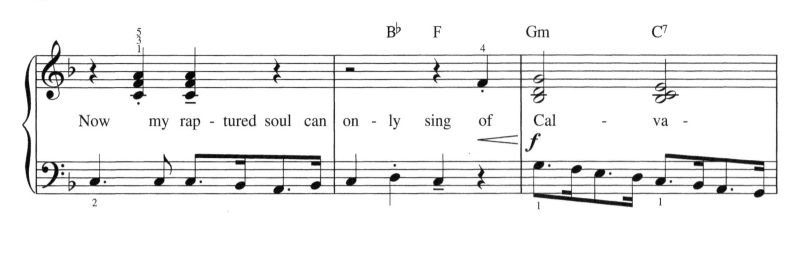

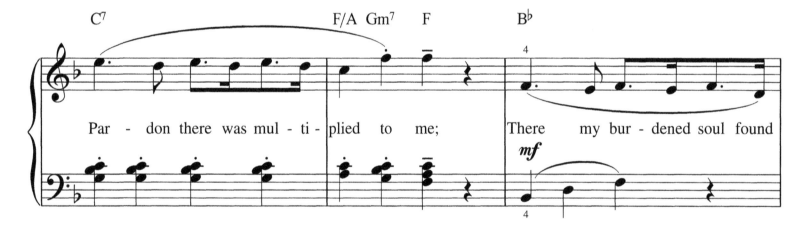

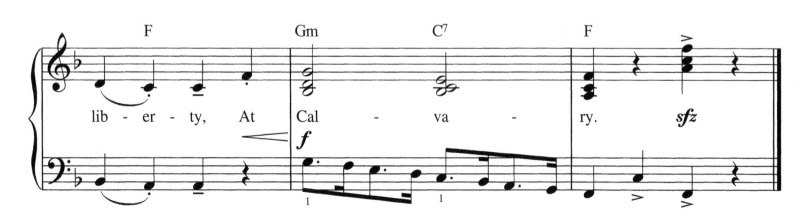

CHURCH IN THE WILDWOOD

Words and Music by DR. WILLIAM S. PITTS
Arranged by Phillip Keveren

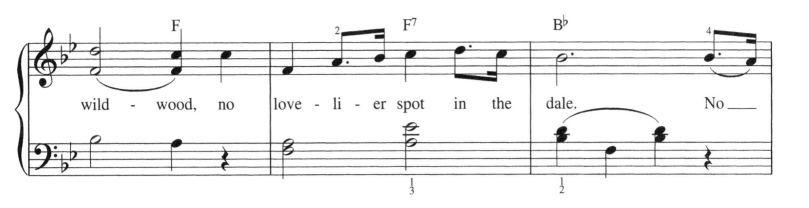

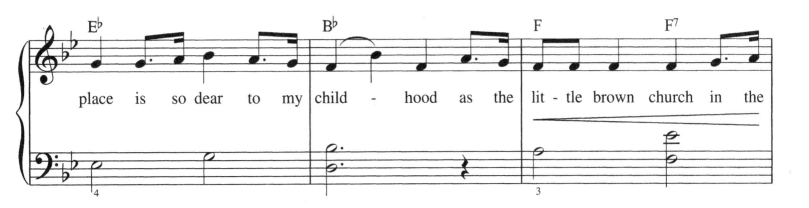

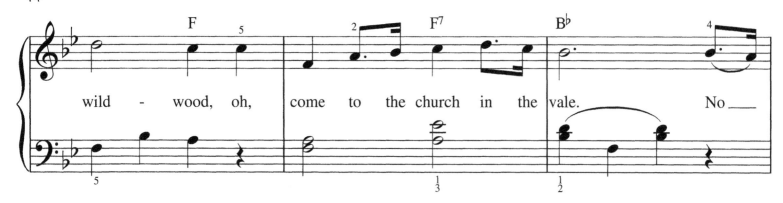

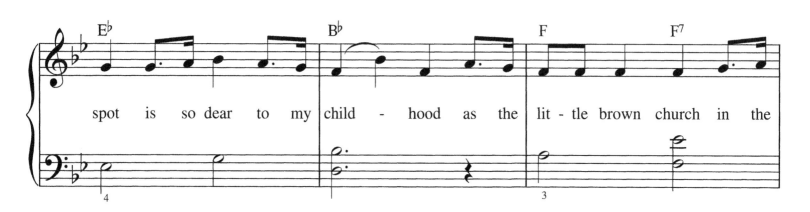

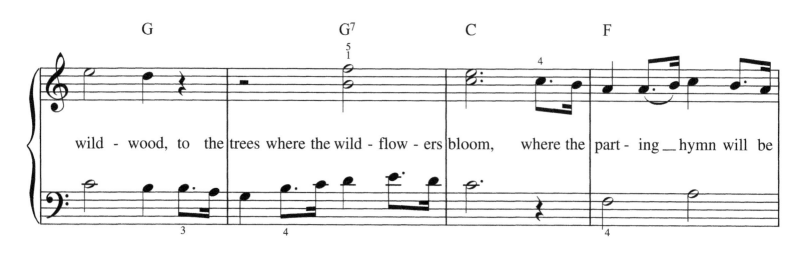

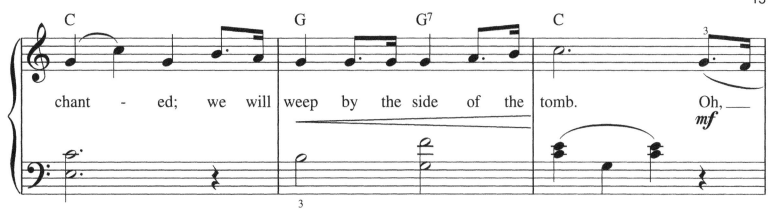

chant - ed; we will weep by the side of the tomb. Oh, ___

come, come, come, come, come to the church in the wild - wood, oh,

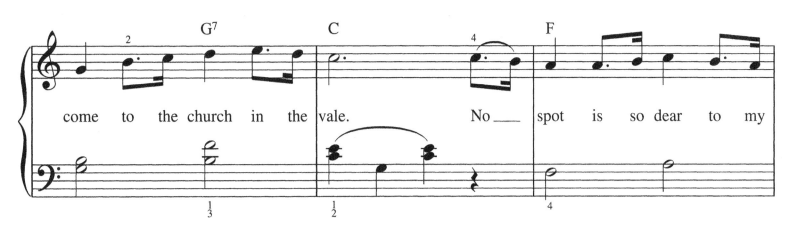

come to the church in the vale. No ___ spot is so dear to my

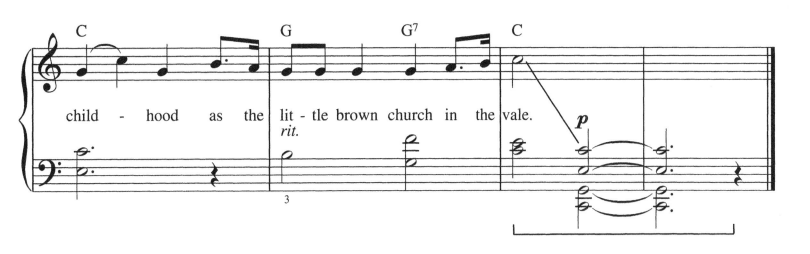

child - hood as the lit - tle brown church in the vale.

HIS EYE IS ON THE SPARROW

Words by CIVILLA D. MARTIN
Music by CHARLES H. GABRIEL
Arranged by Phillip Keveren

I HAVE DECIDED TO FOLLOW JESUS

Folk Melody from India
Adapted by AUILA READ
Arranged by Phillip Keveren

With relaxed Country flair

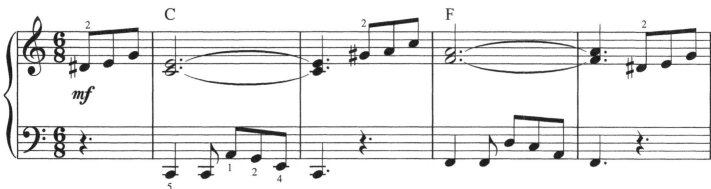

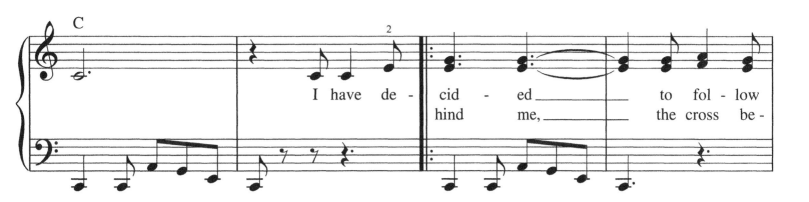

I have de - cid - ed _____ to fol - low
hind me, _____ the cross be -

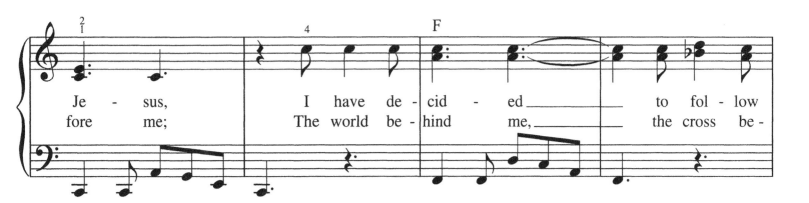

Je - sus,
fore me;
I have de - cid - ed _____ to fol - low
The world be - hind me, _____ the cross be -

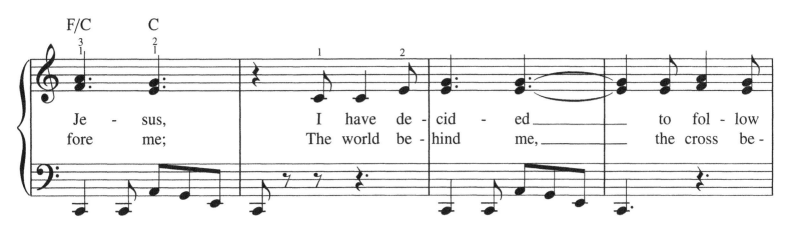

Je - sus,
fore me;
I have de - cid - ed _____ to fol - low
The world be - hind me, _____ the cross be -

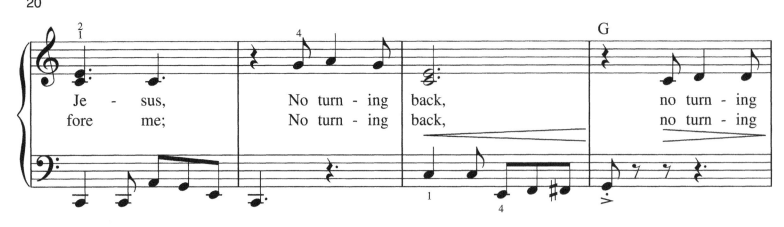

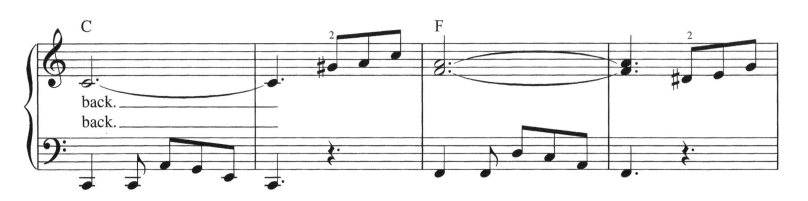

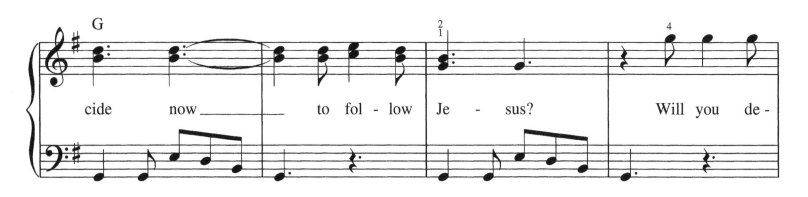

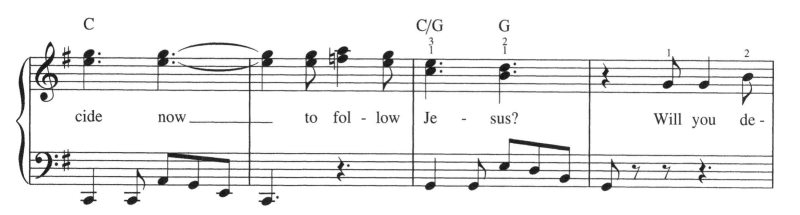

cide now _____ _____ to fol - low Je - sus? Will you de -

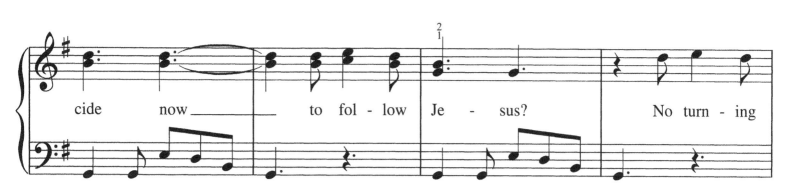

cide now _____ _____ to fol - low Je - sus? No turn - ing

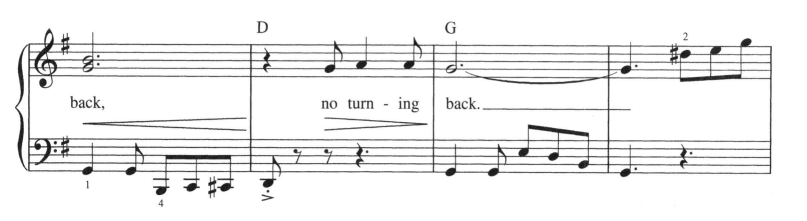

back, no turn - ing back. _____ _____

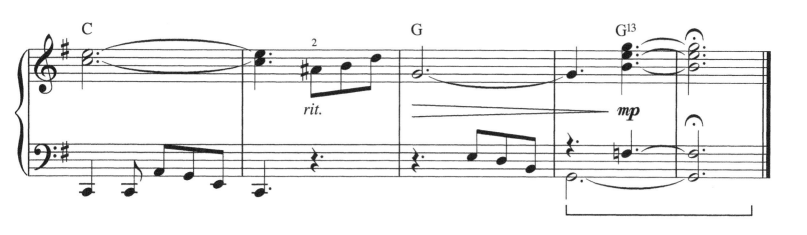

rit. *mp*

I'VE GOT PEACE LIKE A RIVER

Traditional
Arranged by Phillip Keveren

Slowly, soulfully

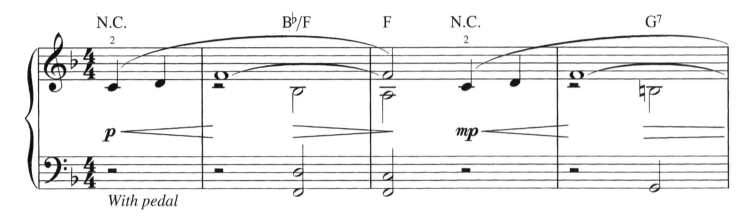

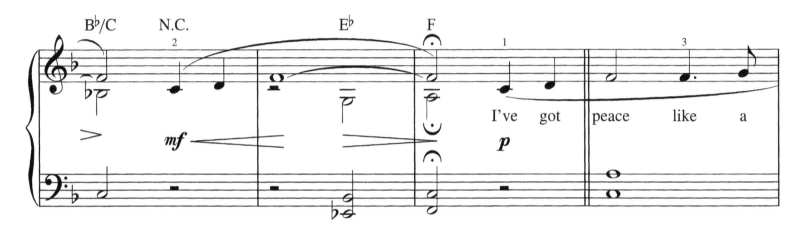

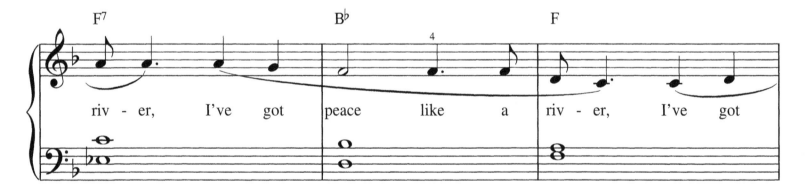

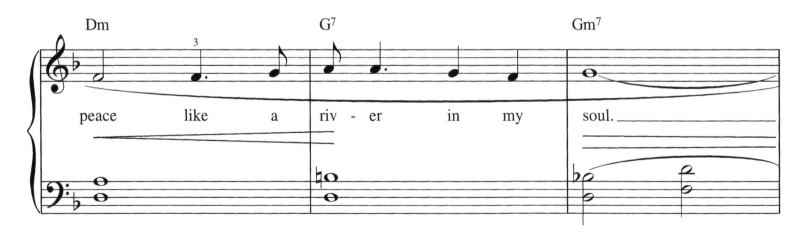

JUST A CLOSER WALK WITH THEE

Traditional
Adapted by KENNETH MORRIS
Arranged by Phillip Keveren

JESUS IS THE SWEETEST
NAME I KNOW

Words and Music by LELA LONG
Arranged by Phillip Keveren

just the same — as His love - ly name, And

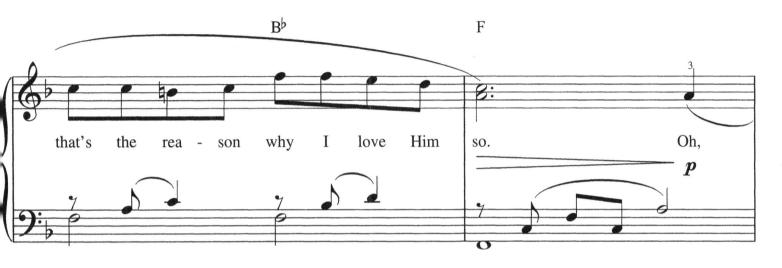

that's the rea - son why I love Him so. Oh,

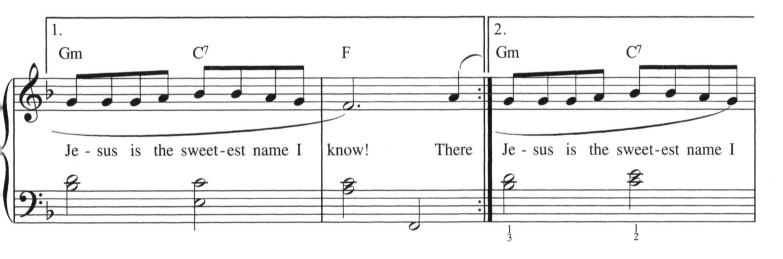

1.
Je - sus is the sweet-est name I know! There

2.
Je - sus is the sweet-est name I

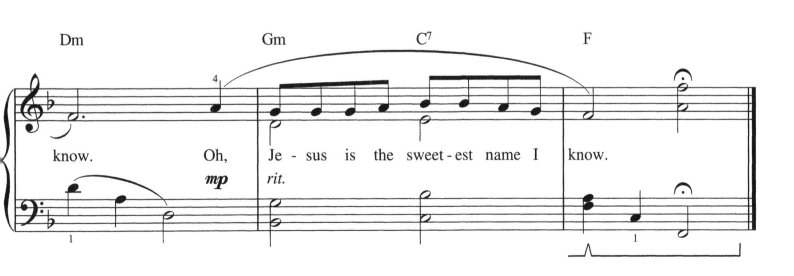

know. Oh, Je - sus is the sweet-est name I know.

LEANING ON THE EVERLASTING ARMS

Words by ELISHA A. HOFFMAN
Music by ANTHONY J. SHOWALTER
Arranged by Phillip Keveren

NOTHING BUT THE BLOOD

Words and Music by ROBERT LOWRY
Arranged by Phillip Keveren

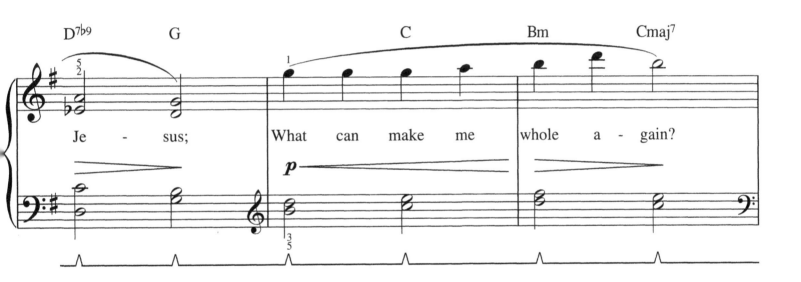

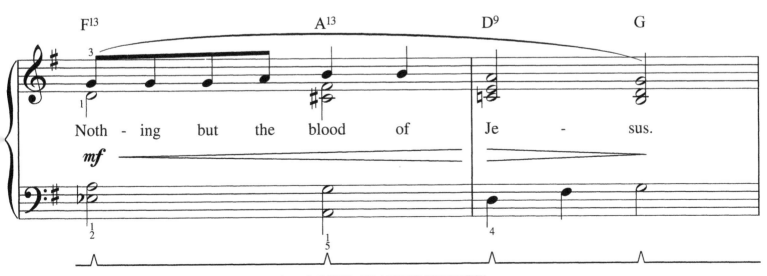

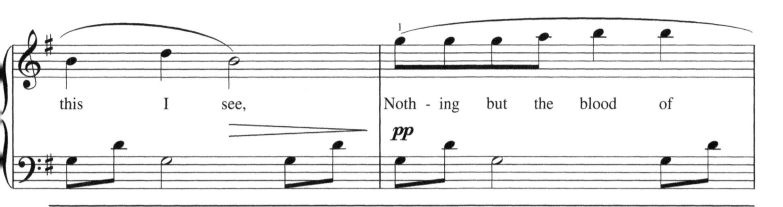

this   I   see,   Noth - ing   but   the   blood   of

pp

Je - sus;   For   my   cleans - ing,   this   my   plea,

mp   *mf*

ped. continuously

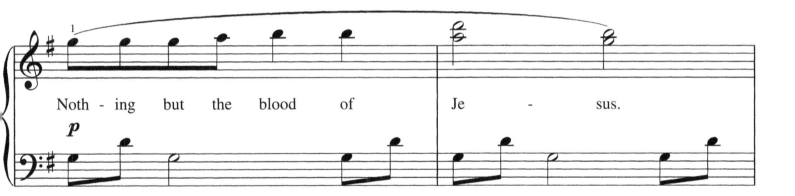

Noth - ing   but   the   blood   of   Je - sus.

p

D.S. al Fine

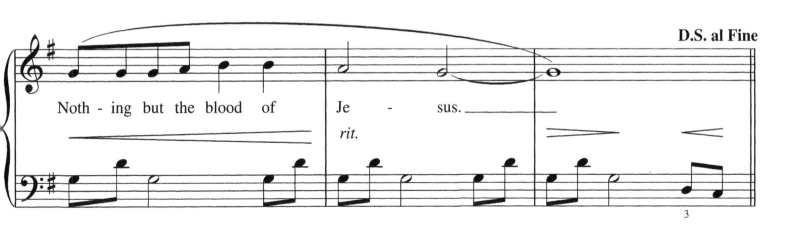

Noth - ing but the blood of   Je - sus.

rit.

3

PRECIOUS MEMORIES

Words and Music by J.B.F. WRIGHT
Arranged by Phillip Keveren

How they ev - er flood my soul._____ In the still - ness

of the mid - night, Pre - cious sa - cred scenes un - fold.

1. 2.

Very slowly

REVIVE US AGAIN

Words by WILLIAM P. MacKAY
Music by JOHN J. HUSBAND
Arranged by Phillip Keveren

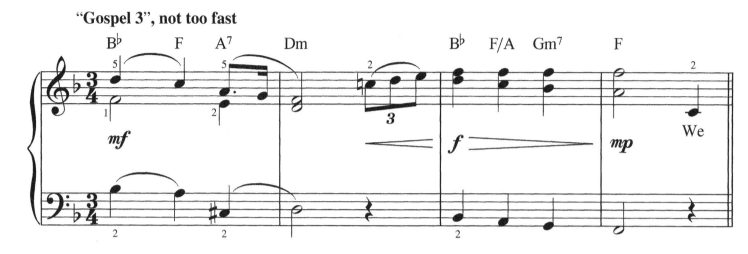

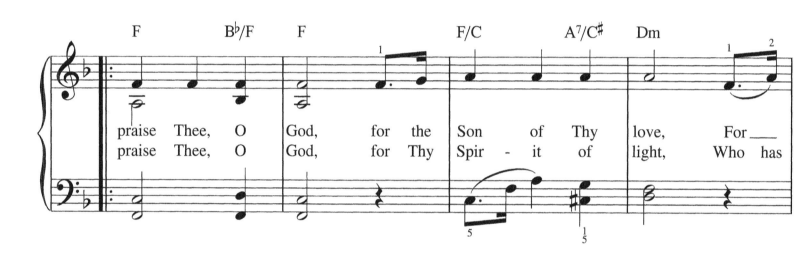

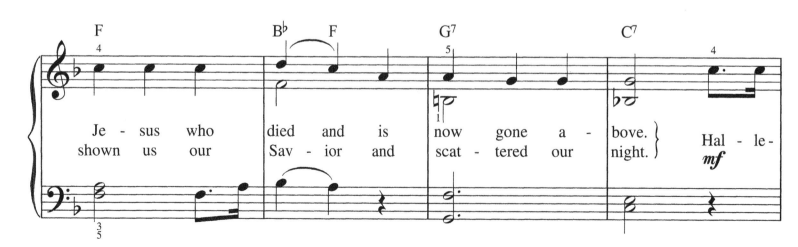

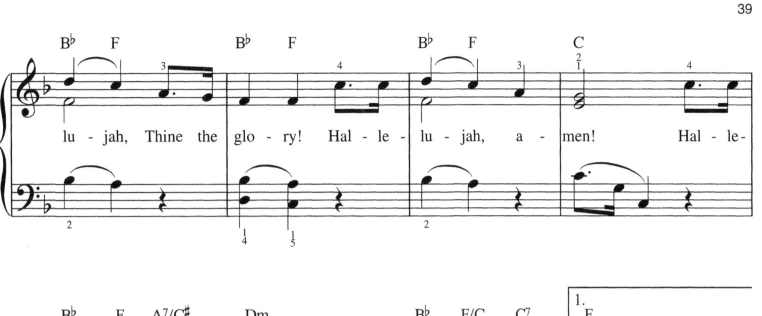

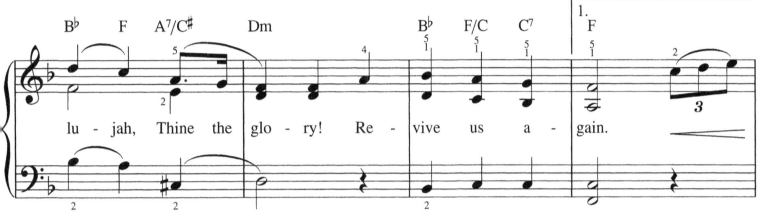

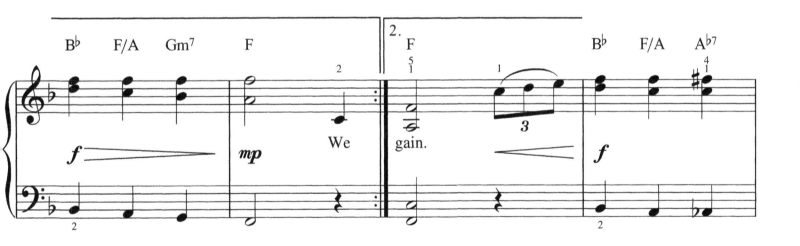

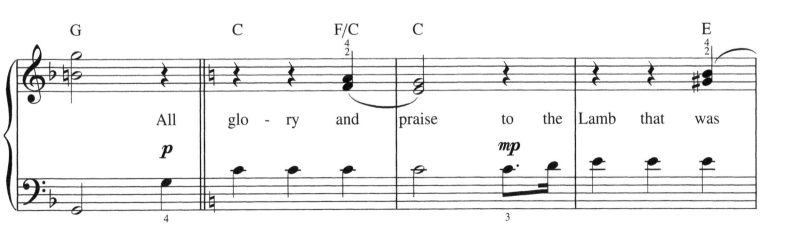

slain, Who has borne all our sins and has cleansed ev - 'ry

stain. Hal - le - lu - jah, Thine the glo - ry! Hal - le - lu - jah, a -

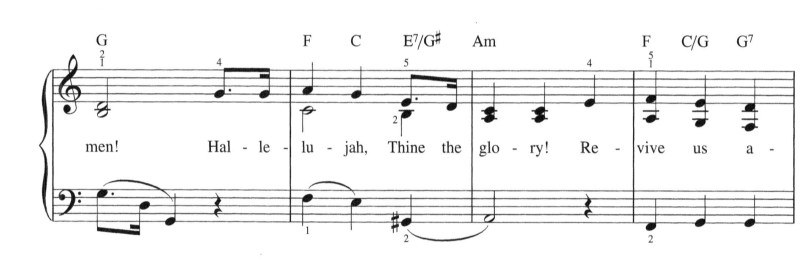

men! Hal - le - lu - jah, Thine the glo - ry! Re - vive us a -

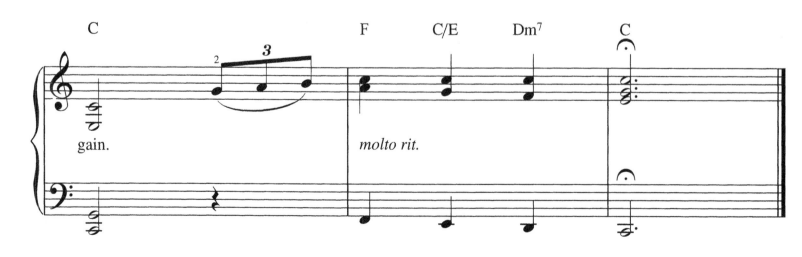

gain.

molto rit.

WHEN WE ALL GET TO HEAVEN

Words by ELIZA E. HEWITT
Music by EMILY D. WILSON
Arranged by Phillip Keveren

Joyous March

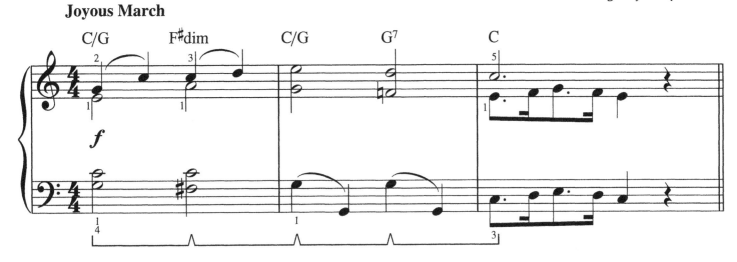

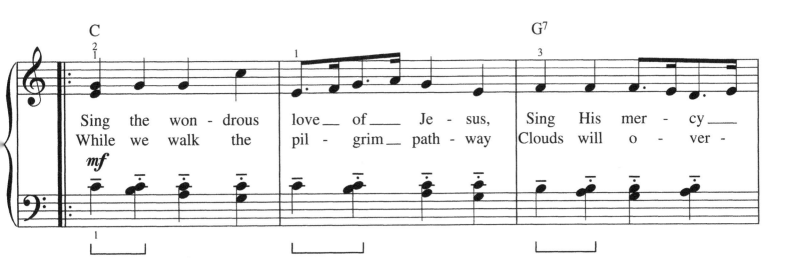

Sing the won - drous love __ of __ Je - sus,
While we walk the pil - grim __ path - way

Sing His mer - cy __
Clouds will o - ver -

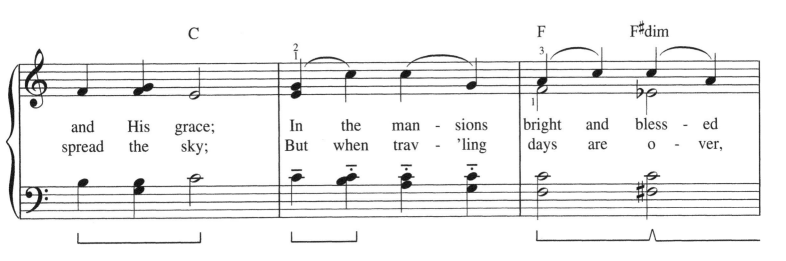

and His grace;
spread the sky;

In the man - sions bright and bless - ed
But when trav - 'ling days are o - ver,

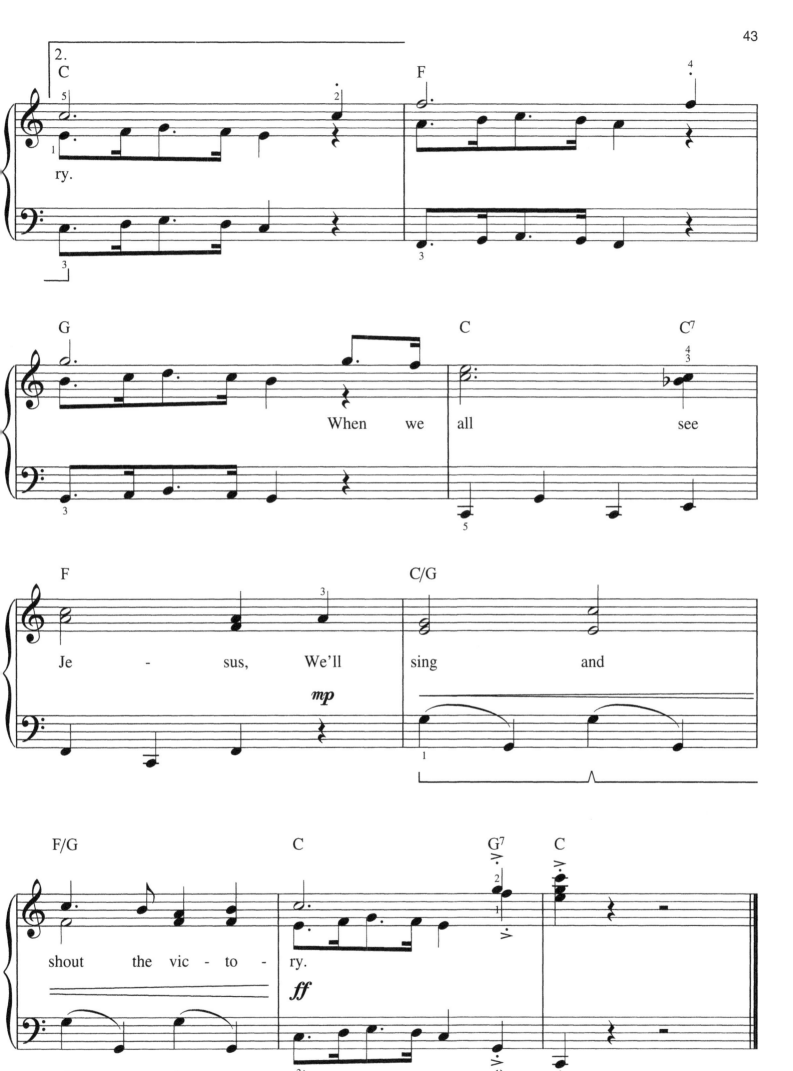

SHALL WE GATHER AT THE RIVER?

Words and Music by ROBERT LOWRY
Arranged by Phillip Keveren

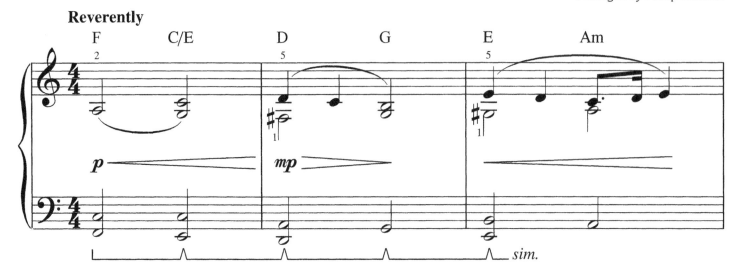

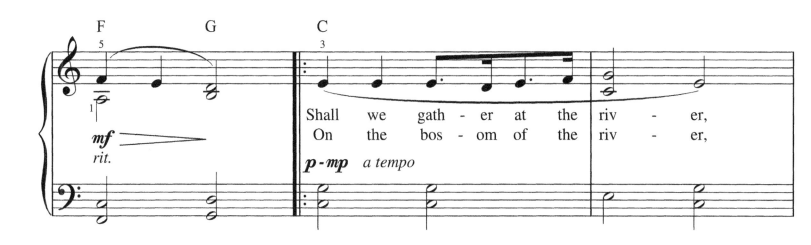

Shall we gath - er at the riv - er,
On the bos - om of the riv - er,

Where bright an - gel feet have trod;_____ With its crys - tal tide for-
Where the Sav - ior King we own,_____ We shall meet, and sor - row

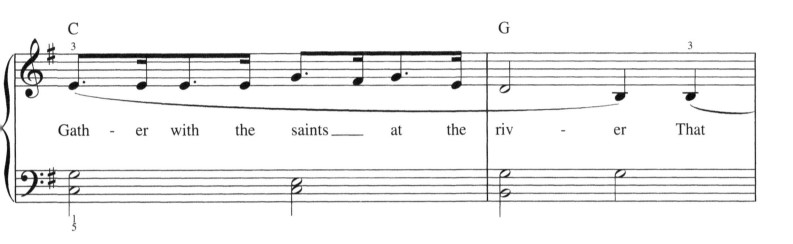

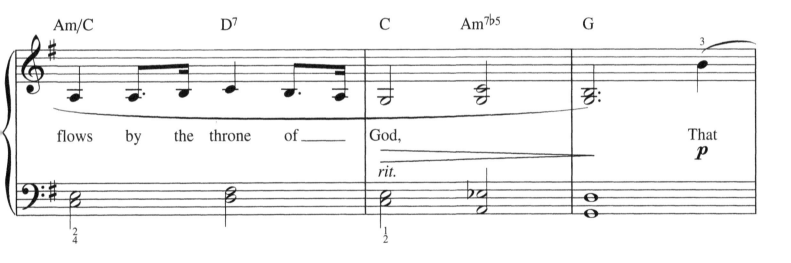

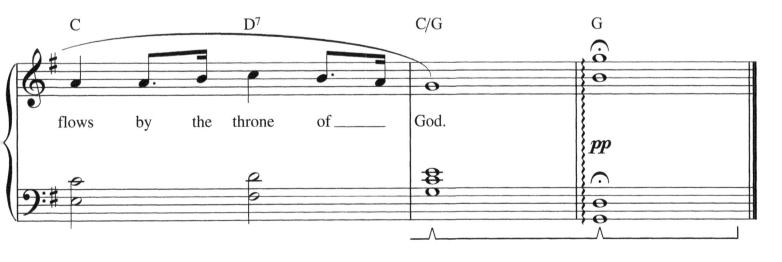

THERE IS POWER IN THE BLOOD

Words and Music by LEWIS E. JONES
Arranged by Phillip Keveren

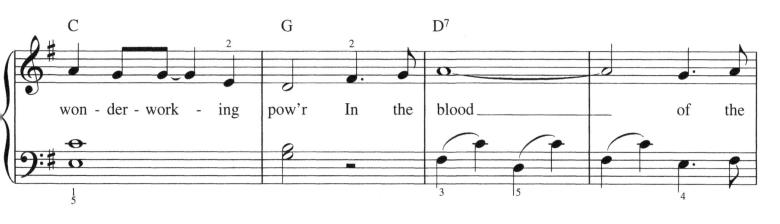

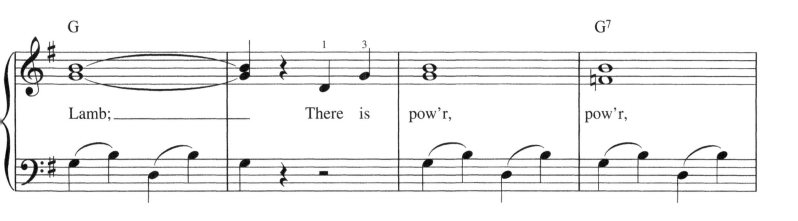

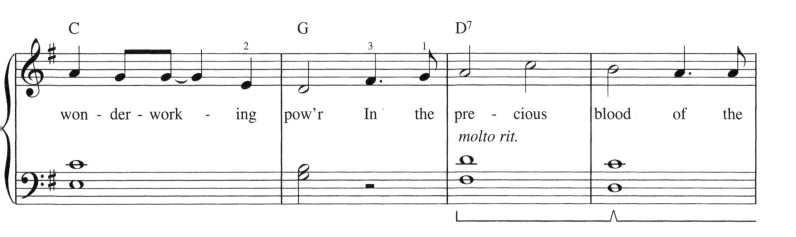

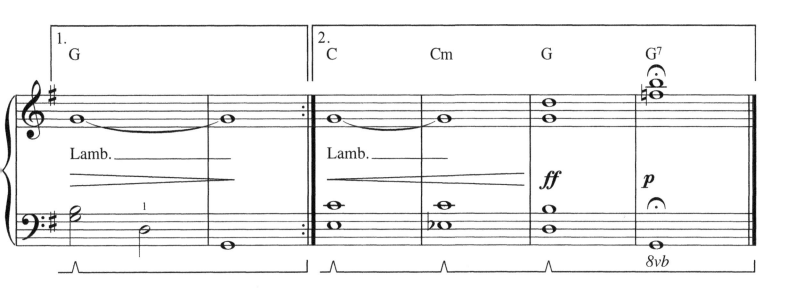

WHISPERING HOPE

Words and Music by ALICE HAWTHORNE
Arranged by Phillip Keveren

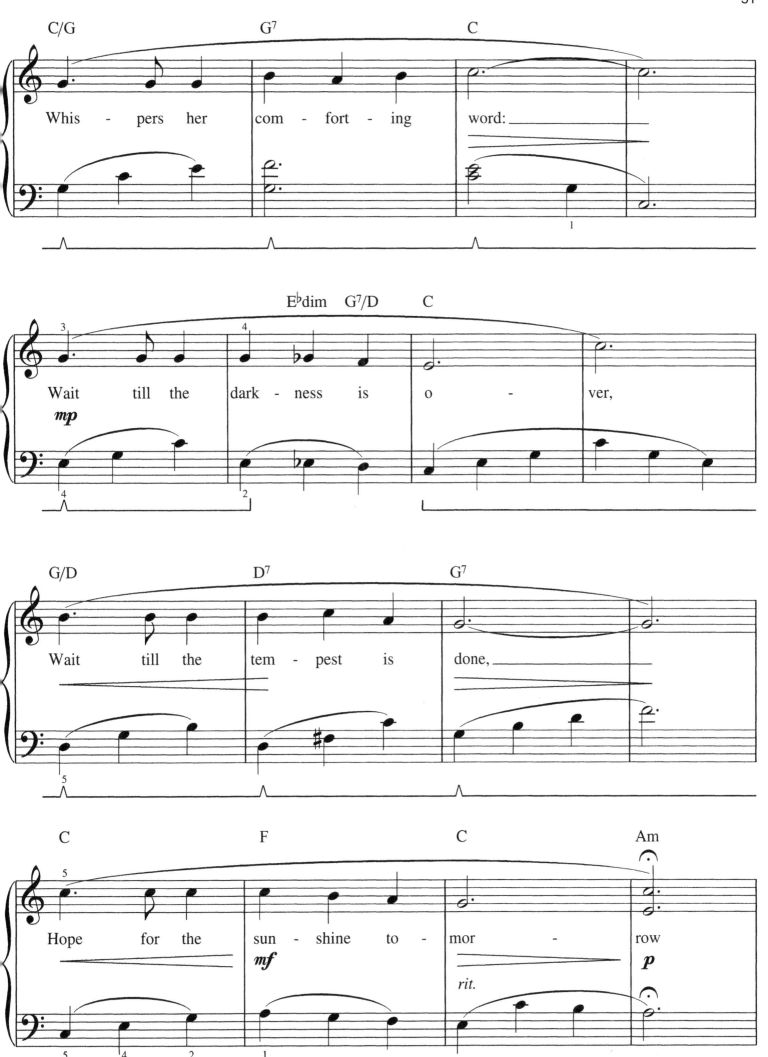

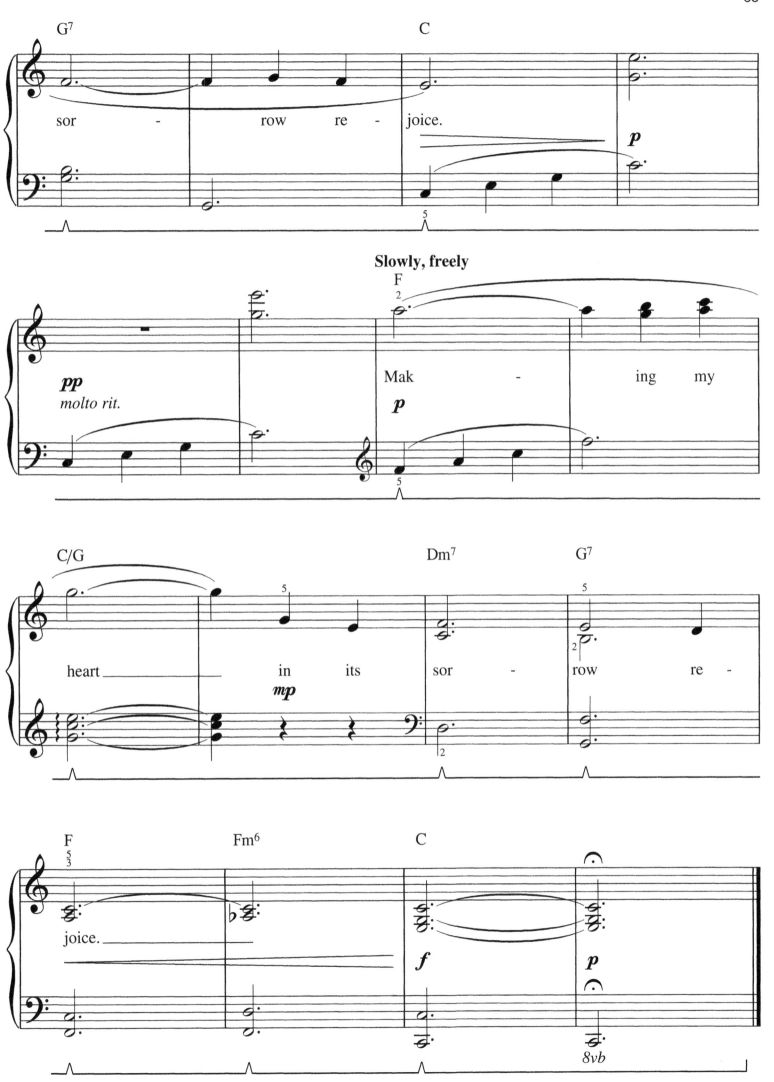

WONDERFUL PEACE

Words by W.D. CORNELL
Music by W.G. COOPER
Arranged by Phillip Keveren

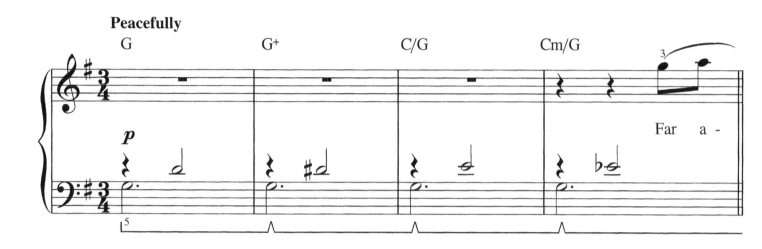

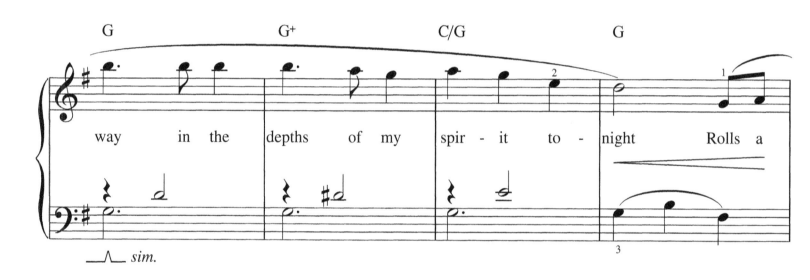

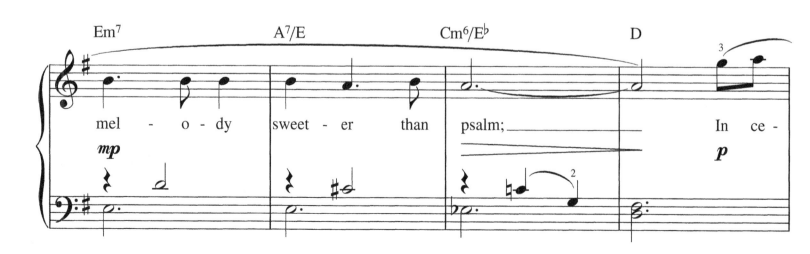

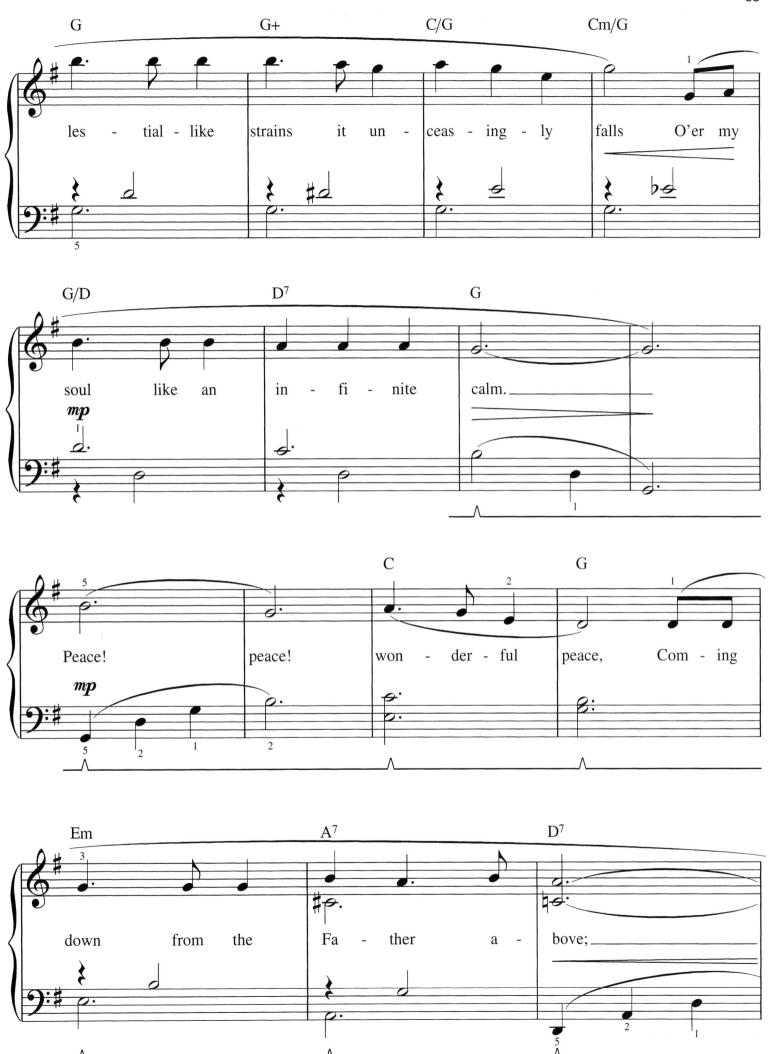